BLUEPRINT

A FOUNDATION OF HOPE WHEN HOME IS LOST

By

Wade Souza

Blueprint: A Foundation of Hope When Home is Lost
ISBN: 9781093753325

Religion / Christian Ministry / Discipleship
Religion / Christian Life / Spiritual Growth

DEDICATION

Blueprint is dedicated in loving memory of Welcome Home's first homeless disciple, Clyde Moses.

ACKNOWLEDGMENTS

All glory to God for ransoming me, rescuing me, and repurposing me to live for Him. *Blueprint* is a testimony of what He can do in His people, through His people, and in spite of His people. He has used *Blueprint* to stretch, strengthen, and shape me throughout this process, while impacting others along the way.

Many hours, hearts, and hands went into introducing and producing *Blueprint*...

I thank my wife, Lindsey, for her incredible patience and encouragement throughout the writing and editing process. You are an amazing partner in our ministry of marriage!

I thank my dear friend, John Almquist, who modeled Christlikeness and mentored me throughout my first years of serving the homeless at Welcome Home. He helped me discover and develop the gifts God has entrusted to me, while encouraging me to create *Blueprint*.

I thank all of the volunteers at Welcome Home, past and present, who have "spurred me on towards love and good deeds." As fellow servants of Christ, your faithfulness and friendship mean more to me than I can succinctly express. Special thanks to Jordan Whetsell for his role in editing *Blueprint*, as well as Ian Head and Wesley Mercer for their roles as mentors.

I thank all of the men and women we have served at Welcome Home. I am certain you have taught me more than I have taught you. What a joy our journey has been together! Special thanks to Samuel, Tony, Okeke, Chibueze, Daniel, and the many others who have experienced *Blueprint* together.

I thank Watermark Community Church for its support, leadership, and generosity, especially Jeff Ward and the External Focus Team. Thanks for making room for us!

I thank Adorah Tidwell and the team at UImpact that made this resource a reality by guiding me through my first publication. I could not have done it without you!

I thank you, the reader, for your willingness to pick up *Blueprint* and grow in your relationship with Jesus Christ. I hope God will use this tool for His glory, your good, and the good of others.

Thanks!

Wade Souza

TABLE OF CONTENTS

INTRODUCTION

Dear Friend,

First, let us tell you the story of the book you now hold in your hands. *Blueprint* began as a response to the miraculous work of God at Welcome Home, our local homeless ministry in Dallas, Texas. As the men and women we served deepened in their desire to become disciples of Christ, we considered how to most effectively meet such a God-honoring demand. The resources available for homeless discipleship largely underwhelmed us. In response, we have crafted a curriculum to specifically teach the foundations of Christianity to souls on the streets, in the shelter, in rehab, or in any other season of transition. *Blueprint* is not the answer for what ails you, Jesus Christ is. Therefore, we designed *Blueprint* to provide ample kindling for God to instill and ignite your faith in Him.

We celebrate your desire to grow in knowledge and understanding of the one true God. By His power and grace, our sincerest prayer would be for the biblical truths and wisdom shared in *Blueprint* to fill your soul with hope, regardless of where you lay your head at night. As countless self-help books litter library and bookstore shelves, we wholeheartedly believe the Bible provides the only perfect blueprint for life, peace, and purpose -- and that blueprint is Jesus Christ.

In 1 Corinthians 3:11, Paul outlines our blueprint, "For no one can lay any foundation other than the one already laid, which is Jesus Christ." Therefore, the goal of *Blueprint* is two-fold:

To diagnose and demolish existing foundations threatening your spiritual, physical, and emotional welfare.

To develop and deepen in an abiding relationship with Jesus Christ.

With the help of the Holy Spirit and the guidance of your mentor, *Blueprint* will allow you to not only see and flee the destructive consequences of your sin, but also fall more in love with God. We pray

His perfect, unending love will compel you to faithfully respond to His will for your life, one decision at a time.

Wherever you are and whatever you are experiencing, we plead with God to grow your faith and trust in Him. Our hope is for the good news of Jesus's death and resurrection to transform your heart and mind, as you grasp the unbelievable lengths God has gone to reveal how much He loves you.

As Paul triumphantly declares in Romans 5:8, "But God demonstrates His own love for us in this: While we were still sinners, Christ died for us." No matter who you are, God has not given up on you. No matter where you are, God has not forgotten you. No matter what you've done, God can forgive you. You are loved. Your life is worth living. Freedom, healing, and fulfillment are freely offered through the pierced hands of Jesus Christ. We pray you will trust Him to lead you and guide you for the rest of your life-- for God's glory, for your good, and for the good of those around you.

Sincerely,

Wade Souza and the Welcome Home family

SAMUEL'S STORY:

OUR FIRST BLUEPRINT GRADUATE

Before you begin, we would love to share the amazing story of our first *Blueprint* graduate, Samuel! Samuel was born and raised in Liberia. At 9 years old, Samuel was tragically captured and trained as a child solider amidst his homeland's bloody civil war. Samuel experienced countless forms of abuse and daily witnessed the horrors of war, hatred, and violence. He spent 20 years disconnected from his family. At one point,

Samuel escaped, only to be recaptured and brutally beaten—to the point his sight progressively waned. As a blind man, Samuel became an advocate for the disabled community and served as an itinerant political and social activist.

In 2016, Samuel arrived in Dallas, Texas. During his stay at the Salvation Army, he took a persistent friend's advice and hopped on the Welcome Home van to attend church and share a meal. Far from home, Welcome Home soon became family to Samuel. His eagerness to grow spiritually (along with others like him) prompted our team to produce the first draft of our homeless discipleship program, *Blueprint*. Samuel not only graduated *Blueprint*, but completed our church's 12-step recovery program, attends college in Dallas, and now lives in his own apartment. He is a member of Watermark Community Church and continues to grow in his faith through community, spiritual training, service, and evangelism.

How Did Blueprint Impact Samuel?

"Although I was homeless, the biblical truths in *Blueprint* helped me grow and better endure my trials. *Blueprint* was eye-opening, as I learned the love of Jesus Christ and experienced the love of my mentors, my brothers in Christ. I better understood the consequences of my rebellion against God, but also the blessing and transformation possible through following Him. Homelessness was not easy. I was lost, lonely, and had unmet physical and spiritual needs. It was a very difficult environment to endure. However, through *Blueprint* I grew in my relationship with Jesus Christ and found rest for my soul in Him. I want people to understand how the Word of God reveals the right path for life, one where we can remain connected to our Savior's love. For through God's grace, we find healing, help, and hope, while also finding our true identity."

OVERVIEW

We thank you for choosing *Blueprint* to help you faithfully live out Jesus's example, and His command in Matthew 28:19 to "make disciples of all nations." In order to most effectively utilize *Blueprint*, here is a quick overview of the program, along with a few helpful suggestions and strategies:

BLUEPRINT Is:

- A 10-week, 10-lesson discipleship program designed to teach the foundational truths of Christianity to men and women on the streets, in a shelter, or in recovery.
- Focused on the disciple's spiritual needs, beliefs, and practices, to encourage, educate, equip, and empower the disciple, as he/she pursues practical steps of rehabilitation, responsibility, and restoration.
- Composed of homework to facilitate research, reflection, and repentance.
- We believe the Bible is the eternal, inspired Word of God: trustworthy, authoritative, and transformative.
- We believe salvation is through faith alone, by grace alone, in Christ alone.

BLUEPRINT Is Not:

- Comprehensive, but serves as an introductory resource to the Christian faith.
- A substitute for local church membership, but serves as a stepping-stone and supplement to deepen fellowship with God and His people.
- Easy, but requires initiative, commitment, and discipline.
- Intended to fix your practical and physical needs, but point you to the One who can strengthen you and sustain in all circumstances.

Discuss: What hopes do you have as you begin *Blueprint*?

BEST PRACTICES

Blueprint is most effective when completed as partners or in a group setting with a spiritually-mature mentor(s). The Bible establishes relationships as the context for discipleship, characterized by accountability, encouragement, teaching, prayer, and correction. Honesty, humility, discipline, and dependence provide the fertile soil for the Holy Spirit and Scriptures to bear fruit in all participants.

Blueprint is a 10-week Bible study, which includes a mentor or group meeting each week (and encouragement between meetings). Each participant should complete their homework before each meeting. Each meeting should last 1 to 1.5 hours, depending on the mentor's knowledge and command, the disciple's engagement, and the level of additional conversation, counsel, encouragement, or correction that occurs. Given the personal nature of the study, men should mentor men and women should mentor women.

We Also Suggest:

- The mentor completes each week's lesson and homework.
- The mentor models vulnerability, authenticity, and confession of sin.
- The mentor directs the flow of the meetings.
- The mentor and disciples use each lesson's "Bible Reference Sheet" for easy and efficient passage reference.
- For groups, incorporate a hymn (page 71) each week before the lesson, as an opportunity to worship.
- Participants do not procrastinate and wait until the last minute to complete the homework.
- The mentor celebrates and encourages the disciple/group throughout the course, especially upon completion!

BLUEPRINT #1: SALVATION

Homelss, But Not Hopeless

"For what I received I passed on to you as of first importance: that Christ died for our sins according to the Scriptures, that he was buried, that he was raised on the third day according to the Scriptures," 1 Cor. 15:3-4

As Paul teaches in the above passage, deliverance from our sins through Jesus Christ's death and resurrection is of utmost importance in the Christian faith. As the wise builder builds on a solid foundation, the Bible teaches that Jesus Christ is the only foundation worthy of our faith (1 Cor. 3:11)*. Regardless of social class, skin color, or sin struggle, salvation is only possible through faith in Jesus Christ (Acts 4:12), by the power of the Holy Spirit (Rom. 8:10-11). Apart from faith in Christ, a right relationship with God, forgiveness, and eternal life remain impossible.

If you are homeless, salvation through faith in Jesus Christ means you are never eternally hopeless, helpless, or homeless. No matter what you have done or what you have been through in your life, Jesus freely offers you forgiveness for every sin—past, present, and future. If you believe in Him, then this broken world of injustice, violence, suffering, disease, and death is not your permanent home (Phil. 3:20-21). Someday, all believers will live in perfect harmony in a new heaven and a new earth with God, under the perfect reign of Jesus Christ (Rev. 21:1-3). Every source and form of sin, sorrow, and death (Rev. 21:4) will be no more, forevermore. The promise of God to deliver you to this perfect world in the future means you can endure the trials of today with perspective, perseverance, and hope (2 Tim. 4:17-18).

Evil is not winning. Your suffering is not only temporary, but purposeful on the path of obedience (2 Cor. 4:17). One day, Jesus will right every wrong in this broken world and gloriously redeem every pain you have ever experienced (Rom. 8:28). Therefore, not only are you not hopeless, but you are not helpless. You may feel overwhelmed, but you are not alone (Heb. 13:5). If you are a true believer in Christ, you have received the Spirit of God (Rom. 5:3-5), the transforming truth of the Word of God (Josh. 1:8-9), and the support of the family of God (Gal. 6:2). You are not alone. God and His people can equip you and empower you to endure every trial, trouble, and temptation along the way, as you walk by faith in Him.

Discuss: What most comforts you from the previous reading?

* Verse references are included for further personal study.

GOD'S BLUEPRINT: A Summary of Salvation

Salvation refers to God's gracious rescue and restoration of fallen sinners through faith in Jesus Christ. Later in this lesson, you will learn *The Bridge Illustration*, which will walk you through His perfect plan to save believers from sin, death, and hell and save believers for the blessing of forever fellowship with Him. Because all people have rebelled against an eternal and holy God (Rom. 3:23), there exists an eternal separation between God and man (Is. 59:2). Not only does sin make a right relationship with God impossible, but sin is responsible for all of the suffering, sickness, death, and destruction in the world (Rom. 6:23). On your own, there is nothing you can do to bridge this eternal gap - not good intentions, not good deeds, not church attendance (Eph. 2:8-9). Without God's help, you cannot save yourself. That's the bad news...

However, that's not the end of His story, or yours...

The good news is the Gospel.

The Gospel declares that because of His perfect love, God the Father sent His one and only Son Jesus Christ to rescue, redeem, and restore sinners through faith (John 3:16). Fully man, yet fully God, Jesus lived the perfect life that you and I never could (Col. 1:15). As our sinless substitute (Hebr. 4:15), He died the death we deserved, and paid the penalty for our sins (1 Pet. 3:18). On the third day, Jesus rose from the dead. Forty days later, He ascended into heaven and sits at the right hand of God the Father (Acts 1:3, 1 Pet. 3:22).

Therefore, Jesus Christ is the only true bridge between God and man (1 Tim. 2:5). By grace, God grants His Holy Spirit to secure salvation for all believers (Eph. 1:13), which allows us to cross over from death to life (John 5:24) and receive adoption into the family of God (Rom. 8:14-15). In Christ, all believers are forever forgiven (Col. 1:13-14), no longer under condemnation (Rom. 8:1), and have access to God through prayer (Rom. 5:2). Only those who trust in Jesus Christ as their Lord and Savior (Rom. 10:9-10) receive God's free gift of salvation (Eph. 2:8-9). Salvation is not possible through any other means, except by grace alone, through faith alone, in Christ alone.

Discuss: What words would you use to describe yourself? What words would you use to describe God?

WEEK 1 BIBLE REFERENCES

Here are the passages we'll use during today's lesson. Refer to these pages, as needed.

John 5:24 - "Very truly I tell you, whoever hears my word and believes him who sent me has eternal life and will not be judged but has crossed over from death to life."

Romans 3:23 - "for all have sinned and fall short of the glory of God,"

Romans 6:23 - "For the wages of sin is death, but the gift of God is eternal life in Christ Jesus our Lord."

Hebrews 9:27 - "Just as people are destined to die once, and after that to face judgment,"

Romans 5:8 - "But God demonstrates his own love for us in this: While we were still sinners, Christ died for us."

John 3:16 – "For God so loved the world that he gave his one and only Son, that whoever believes in Him shall not perish but have eternal life."

Ephesians 2:8-9 – "For it is by grace you have been saved, through faith—and this is not from yourselves, it is the gift of God—not by works, so that no one can boast."

Closing Prayer: Ephesians 3:14-21

BUILDING BLOCKS: The Bridge Illustration

The Bridge Illustration serves as a simple, yet powerful teaching tool to better understand and share the good news of the Gospel. Through these six verses, the Bible helps us understand not only our sinfulness and the consequences of sin, but also the surpassing love of God. He offers a perfect plan of rescue and restoration to us through faith in Jesus Christ. Our salvation was made possible through Christ's perfect life, death, and resurrection. As Jesus summarizes in John 5:24, "Very truly I tell you, whoever hears my word and believes him who sent me has eternal life and will not be judged but has crossed over from death to life."

Read each summary phrase and the corresponding verse (from your Week 1 Bible Cheat Sheet). Discuss what these verses tell you about yourself and God.

Man's Separation
1. All have sinned. (Romans 3:23)
2. All deserve death. (Romans 6:23)
3. All face judgment. (Hebrews 9:27)

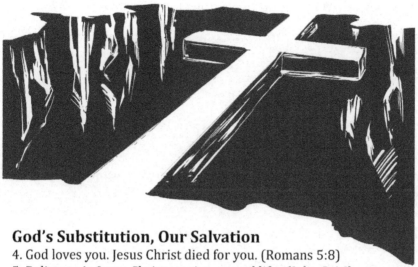

God's Substitution, Our Salvation
4. God loves you. Jesus Christ died for you. (Romans 5:8)
5. Believers in Jesus Christ receive eternal life. (John 3:16)
6. Salvation is not by works, but by grace, through faith in Christ. (Ephesians 2:8-9)

CLOSING PRAYER: Ephesians 3:14-21

MEMORY VERSE: Salvation (Homework)

Memorize the following verse to recite at your next mentor meeting.

"For it is by grace you have been saved, through faith—and this is not from yourselves, it is the gift of God— not by works, so that no one can boast." Ephesians 2:8-9

INSPECTION: Salvation (Homework)

Complete this section of personal assessment on your own, prior to the next meeting.

What is the Gospel? What good news does the Gospel declare?

If you died today, on a scale of 1-10, how certain are you that you would go to heaven? Circle your answer, 10 = absolutely certain.

1   2   3   4   5   6   7   8   9   10

Explain why you chose that number.

Do you believe faith in Jesus Christ is the only way to heaven? Why or why not?

From what did Jesus Christ personally save you? What specific sins or sin struggles did Jesus Christ pay the penalty for for you?

What is most challenging about your current situation?

What hope does the Gospel offer to you in your present circumstances?

BLUEPRINT #1: SALVATION

RECITE:

Ephesians 2:8-9

REVIEW:

Inspection: Salvation

WEEK 2 BIBLE REFERENCES

Here are the passages we'll use during today's lesson:

John 3:16-17 – "For God so loved the world that he gave his one and only Son, that whoever believes in him shall not perish but have eternal life. For God did not send his Son into the world to condemn the world, but to save the world through him."

Ephesians 2:8-10 – "For it is by grace you have been saved, through faith–and this is not from yourselves, it is the gift of God– not by works, so that no one can boast. For we are God's handiwork, created in Christ Jesus to do good works, which God prepared in advance for us to do."

Romans 5:1-11 – "Therefore, since we have been justified through faith, we have peace with God through our Lord Jesus Christ, through whom we have gained access by faith into this grace in which we now stand. And we boast in the hope of the glory of God. Not only so, but we also glory in our sufferings, because we know that suffering produces perseverance; perseverance, character; and character, hope. And hope does not put us to shame, because God's love has been poured out into our hearts through the Holy Spirit, who has been given to us. You see, at just the right time, when we were still powerless, Christ died for the ungodly. Very rarely will anyone die for a righteous person, though for a good person someone might possibly dare to die. But God demonstrates his own love for us in this: While we were still sinners, Christ died for us. Since we have now been justified by his blood, how much more shall we be saved from God's wrath through him! For if, while we were God's enemies, we were reconciled to him through the death of his Son, how much more, having been reconciled, shall we be saved through his life! Not only is this so, but we also boast in God through our Lord Jesus Christ, through whom we have now received reconciliation."

John 10:28-29 - "I give them eternal life, and they shall never perish; no one will snatch them out of my hand. My Father, who has given them to me, is greater than all; no one can snatch them out of my Father's hand. I and the Father are one."

John 6:39-40 - "And this is the will of him who sent me, that I shall lose none of all those he has given me, but raise them up at the last day. For my Father's will is that everyone who looks to the Son and believes in him shall have eternal life, and I will raise them up at the last day."

Ephesians 1:13-14 - "And you also were included in Christ when you heard the message of truth, the gospel of your salvation. When you believed, you were marked in him with a seal, the promised Holy Spirit, who is a deposit guaranteeing our inheritance until the redemption of those who are God's possession—to the praise of his glory."

Philippians 1:6 - "being confident of this, that he who began a good work in you will carry it on to completion until the day of Christ Jesus."

John 14:6 - "Jesus answered, 'I am the way and the truth and the life. No one comes to the Father except through me.'"

Acts 4:12 - "Salvation is found in no one else, for there is no other name under heaven given to mankind by which we must be saved."

CLOSING PRAYER: Psalm 13

A FIRM FOUNDATION: Salvation Q&A

Read and discuss each Bible passage with mentor. Write your answers in the space provided.

1. Read John 3:16-17. How can you be certain of God's love?

2. Read Ephesians 2:8-10 to answer the following questions:

    a. How does this passage declare someone is saved?

    b. Can you earn salvation by your own works?

            YES   NO

    c. Is this the same as what you have believed in the past, or different? If different, how?

d. What does grace in this passage mean?

e. Once you are saved, what has God prepared for you to do?

3. **Read Romans 5:6-10. What words does Paul use to describe ALL PEOPLE, apart from receiving salvation through faith in Jesus Christ?**

   a. Romans 5:6 - _____ and

   _____ .

   b. Romans 5:8 - _____ .

   c. Romans 5:10 – God's _____ .

4. **The previous verses paint a bleak picture for the fate of all people, apart from God. Yet, for the believer, that's not the whole story. Through faith in Christ, we are justified through His righteousness; therefore, we receive right standing before God. In Romans 5:1-11, Paul lists some of the amazing blessings all believers receive:**

   Verse 1: Peace with God.
   Verse 2: Access into God's grace and future hope.

Verses 3-4: Perseverance, character, and hope in suffering.
Verse 5: The gift of God's Holy Spirit and His love poured into our hearts.
Verse 8: Assurance of God's love.
Verse 8: Christ's example of how to live and love.
Verse 9: Savlvation from God's wrath.
Verse 10: New life in Christ.
Verse 11: A new relationship with God.

How should the contrast of your old identity apart from Christ and your new identity in Christ change your view of God, yourself, and the way you live?

5. **Once you have been truly saved through faith in Jesus Christ, can you lose your salvation through misbehavior? Read John 10:28-29. Circle your answer.**

   YES, I can lose my salvation.   NO, I cannot lose my salvation.

6. **If you have truly believed in Jesus Christ as your Lord and Savior, why can you not lose your salvation?**

   a. **God's Will:** Read John 6:39-40.
      Truth: It is God's will that no one who believes will be lost.

   b. **God's Seal:** Read Ephesians 1:13-14.
      Truth: All believers are sealed by God's Spirit for eternal life.

c. **God's Promise:** Read Philippians 1:6.
Truth: God will finish what He started and save His people.

7. **Many people believe all religions are equal and lead to the same place.**

    a. According to John 14:6, what did Jesus say is the only way to heaven?

    b. According to Acts 4:12, can salvation be found in anyone or anything other than Christ?

    c. Based on these passages, do you believe faith in Jesus Christ is the only way to heaven?

        YES   NO

CLOSING PRAYER: Psalm 13

MEMORY VERSE: Salvation (Homework)

"For it is by grace you have been saved, through faith—and this is not from yourselves, it is the gift of God— not by works, so that no one can boast." Ephesians 2:8-9

RENOVATION: Salvation (Homework)

Regardless of circumstance, race, or residence, all people are equal in the following ways:

- All people are created by God in His image (Gen. 1:27), possessing dignity and worth.
- All people are separated from God through sin (Rom 3:23).
- All people are invited to experience salvation through faith in Jesus Christ (Rev. 22:17).

However:

- Only believers are united with Christ and receive eternal life (Gal. 2:20).
- All believers are united in Christ, regardless of gender, culture, class, or sin (Gal. 3:28).

As the late evangelist Billy Graham famously declared, "The ground is level at the foot of the cross." No one is more deserving of salvation than anyone else, because "all have sinned and fall short of the glory of God (Rom. 3:23)." In spite of your rebellion, God the Father lovingly sent God the Son, Jesus Christ, to suffer and die for your sins. Through faith in Christ, you receive not only forgiveness, but a new life, new Spirit, new family, new purpose, and new hope.

Embracing your new identity in Christ will allow you to flee from the destruction and despair caused by putting on "false selves," and trying to find life apart from Him. In Christ, you are a daughter or son of the King of Kings. In Christ, God sees you as spotless through the righteousness of His Son. You no longer need to fear man or fear death, for God is with you and your future with Him is secure.

Read Romans 8:31-39. Do you see yourself as loved by God? Why or why not? What does this incredible passage teach you?

What are you most thankful for today?

Salvation does not give you the permission to sin, or the freedom from the responsibility to do what is right. Just because you are saved does not mean you should continue to live however you want (Rom. 6:1-14). Rather, God intends His love to compel you to a life of faithfulness, obedience, and worship.

Paul teaches this truth in Colossians 3:16-17, "Let the message of Christ dwell among you richly as you teach and admonish one another with all wisdom through psalms, hymns, and songs from the Spirit, singing to God with gratitude in your hearts. And whatever you do, whether in word or deed, do it all in the name of the Lord Jesus, giving thanks to God the Father through him." As a Christian, the truth and love of the Gospel is to brightly and boldly shine in you and through you-- in everything you think, say, and do.

What immediate steps will you take to be more responsible, faithful, and obedient as a follower of Jesus Christ?

What could you say to encourage someone in a similar situation as you?

Who can you encourage this week with the "good news" of the Gospel or what you have learned about salvation?

BLUEPRINT #2: SIN

RECITE:

Ephesians 2:8-9

REVIEW:

Renovation: Salvation

Sinful and Homeless, but Not Helpless

Since Adam and Eve sinned in the Garden of Eden, sin and its consequences have corrupted God's once-perfect creation (Rom. 5:12). Few environments display the devastating effects of sin more than life on the streets. As you have witnessed and experienced, sin always leaves a tragic trail of broken people, broken relationships, broken promises, and broken systems in its wake. The lost continue to prey on the lost. The dealer continues to profit off of the addict. Desperation and isolation can plunge the poor deeper and deeper into destruction.

Being homeless is not a sin. However, the existence of sin is responsible for the existence of homelessness. You may or may not have contributed to your current circumstances. While you are not responsible for the sin of others, you are responsible for your own sin and how you respond to others (Gal. 6:7). Homelessness is not an excuse to sin, but a daily opportunity to trust God. With the help of God's Word (and your mentor), you must assess what past and present sins have contributed to your current situation, suffering, and sorrow. God calls you to confess and repent (turn away) from your sin and to follow Him (1 John 1:7-9).

Today's lesson is designed to show you how sin robs you of the life that God intends. Sin does not discriminate, but devours people of all races, cultures, and classes. Although sin impacts all people (Rom. 3:23), Christ remains the hope of all nations (Matt. 12:21). His life, death, and resurrection reveal His superior power and glory over sin, death, and the Devil (Col. 2:14-15).

Likewise, God proclaims His mighty power to rescue His people from the deepest of valleys, "I am the Lord, the God of all mankind. Is anything too hard for me (Jer. 32:27)?" Do not believe the lie that God cannot help you fight an addiction, a specific sin struggle, or help you get off the streets. With God's help, there is no problem too great. With God's help, it is never too late.

Discuss: What sinful choices led to your current situation, or worsened your circumstances?

GOD'S BLUEPRINT: *A Summary of Sin*

Since God created us, He knows what is best for us. Since He loves us, He wants what is best for us (John 3:16). Through the Bible, we learn about Christ—the perfect blueprint. As fully God, yet fully man, Jesus was tempted in all the ways that we have been tempted, yet did not sin (Hebr. 4:15). Christ perfectly modeled full devotion to God and His Word (1 Cor. 10:31). Yet, because we are imperfect sinners, we are unable to perfectly follow Christ's example (Is. 53:6).

Sin is the breaking of God's law (1 John 3:4), which separates us from Him (Is. 59:2). His laws are not just random commands or rules, but direct reflections of His perfect character (Ps. 19:7-9). For example, God does not and cannot lie; therefore, He advises us not to lie. In our world, breaking a law results in a punishment-- possibly a fine, probation, or imprisonment. God, alone, is the perfect Judge. He cannot let evil go unpunished (Deut. 32:4). The penalty for breaking one of His laws is death (Rom. 6:23). Each of us are guilty. Apart from salvation in Christ, we would spend eternity in hell, apart from God and everything good (Matt. 25:46). Unfortunately, there is nothing we can do to cancel the sobering debt our sin demands (Eph. 2:1). Fortunately, everyone who believes in Christ receives total forgiveness of their sins (1 Pet. 1:18-19).

The commands of God are not intended to keep us from fun (Eccl. 2:24-26), or true freedom (1 John 5:3). Rather, God has lovingly issued commands and warnings to protect us from the false promises and pain of seeking life apart from Him. His commands not only warn us of danger, deception, and destruction, but they also invite us to experience true life, love, joy, freedom, and purpose by trusting and obeying in Him (Ps. 19:10).

Think of sin this way… If you fill a glass of water and place a drop of poison in it, there is nothing you can do to restore the new mixture back into pure water. It is contaminated. It is impure. This is our story, apart from His intervention. Sin has corrupted us from the inside out.

In mercy, God sent Jesus Christ to cleanse us from our sins and purify us (Heb. 1:3). Faith unites us with our sinless Savior. As a believer, when God looks at you, He no longer sees your sin and guilt. Instead, He now sees His perfect and righteous Son, who suffered and died to pay the penalty for your sins (2 Cor. 5:21). Though you have been saved, your desire and ability to sin do not go away. However, as a believer, you now have the opportunity to flee sin, follow God, and do what is right.

Discuss: Do you hate sin or just its consequences? What's the difference?

Week 3 Bible REFERENCES

Here are the passages we'll use during today's lesson:

James 1:13-15 - "When tempted, no one should say, "God is tempting me." For God cannot be tempted by evil, nor does he tempt anyone; but each person is tempted when they are dragged away by their own evil desire and enticed. Then, after desire has conceived, it gives birth to sin; and sin, when it is full-grown, gives birth to death."

Closing Prayer: "Create in me a pure heart, O God, and renew a steadfast spirit within me. Do not cast me from your presence or take your Holy Spirit from me. Restore to me the joy of your salvation and grant me a willing spirit, to sustain me." Psalm 51:10-12

BUILDING BLOCKS: "The Deadliest Catch"

The cycle of sin is very similar to a fish attracted to a fisherman's shiny lure. The hungry fish views the lure as a real source of provision, only to sink its teeth into the hook and meet a deadly end. In the same way, Proverbs 14:12 warns, "There is a way that appears to be right, but it ends in death." Oftentimes, we mistakenly believe different things of this world will satisfy us in ways that God never intended and that only God can. When we follow our own fleshly desires and disobey God, we will always find a path of death rather than life and peace (Rom. 8:5-8). It is your flesh that will lead to destruction, not the Lord.

Read James 1:13-15. In this passage, James makes it clear that "God does not tempt you." Instead of pointing the finger at Him or blaming others for your problems, you must "draw the circle" around yourself by accepting responsibility for your evil desires, which led to your disobedience, and the destruction caused by your disobedience.

The following tables present practical examples of the cycle of sin, as well as God's blueprint to break the cycle and prevent more pain from avoidable deadly pursuits.

SAMPLE CYCLE OF SIN: PORNOGRAPHY

Desire	Physical Pleasure, Control, Instant Gratification
Temptation	Pornography
Sin	Lust, Masturbation, Seeking Life Apart from God
Death	Disconnected from God, Spiritual Apathy, Physical Addiction, Uncontrolled Cravings, Unmotivated, Dissatisfaction, Isolation, Guilt, Shame, Unhealthy Real-Life Relationships

SAMPLE CYCLE OF SIN: DRUNKENNESS

Desire	Physical Pleasure/Peer Approval/Escape from Reality, Responsibility
Temptation	Alcohol, Bar, Party/Gathering, Convenience Store
Sin	Drunkenness, Seeking Life Apart from God

Discuss: What did you learn from the two sample cycles of sin to help you better understand the root (cause) and deadly fruit (effect) of your own sinful habits?

GOD'S BLUEPRINT TO BATTLE SIN

Complete Dependence on Christ: "But he said to me, "My grace is sufficient for you, for my power is made perfect in weakness." Therefore I will boast all the more gladly about my weaknesses, so that Christ's power may rest on me." 2 Corinthians 12:9

Be Transformed	"Do not conform to the pattern of this world, but be transformed by the renewing of your mind. Then you will be able to test and approve what God's will is—his good, pleasing and perfect will." Romans 12:2
Flee Sin, Follow God	"No temptation has overtaken you except what is common to mankind. And God is faithful; he will not let you be tempted beyond what you can bear. But when you are tempted, he will also provide a way out so that you can endure it." 1 Corinthians 10:13
Confess Sin	"If we confess our sins, he is faithful and just and will forgive us our sins and purify us from all unrighteousness." 1 John 1:9
Pursue Life	"The thief comes only to steal and kill and destroy; I have come that they may have life, and have it to the full." John 10:10

GOD'S SUPPORT SYSTEM	
God's Spirit	"So I say, walk by the Spirit, and you will not gratify the desires of the flesh." Galatians 5:16
God's Word	"I have hidden your word in my heart that I might not sin against you." Psalm 119:11
God's People	"Remember this: Whoever turns a sinner from the error of their way will save them from death and cover over a multitude of sins." James 5:20
God's Portal (Prayer)	"Until now you have not asked for anything in my name. Ask and you will receive, and your joy will be complete." John 16:24

Discuss:

1) In what ways are you following God's blueprint for victory against sin?
2) What area(s) do you need the most help?
3) What next steps could be taken to make war against the sinful and destructive desires of your flesh?

CLOSING PRAYER: Psalm 51:10-12

MEMORY VERSE: Sin (Homework)

"For the wages of sin is death, but the gift of God is eternal life in Christ Jesus our Lord." Romans 6:23

You will also recite Ephesians 2:8-9 (Salvation: Weeks 1-2).

INSPECTION: Sin (Homework)

Do you agree with Romans 3:23 that "all have sinned and fall short of the glory of God," including you?

YES   NO

Can believers still sin?

YES   NO

What are some of your current sin struggles? Be specific and list as many as possible.

Refer to the "Deadliest Catch" illustration to explore a specific sin struggle you currently face. List the desire, temptation, sin, and death (negative outcome) of your sin.

Desire	
Temptation	
Sin	
Death	

Romans 13:14 commands, "But put on the Lord Jesus Christ, and make no provision for the flesh, to gratify its desires." Are you willing to do whatever it takes to put on Christ, fight temptation, and flee sin? Why or why not?

Refer to "God's Support System" in this lesson's *Building Blocks* illustration. Who/what has God provided to help you battle against temptation?

BLUEPRINT #2: SIN

RECITE:

Romans 6:23
Ephesians 2:8-9

REVIEW:

Inspection: Sin

Week 4 Bible References

Here are the passages we'll use during today's lesson:

1 John 3:4 - "Everyone who sins breaks the law; in fact, sin is lawlessness."

Galatians 5:19-21 - "The acts of the flesh are obvious: sexual immorality, impurity and debauchery; idolatry and witchcraft; hatred, discord, jealousy, fits of rage, selfish ambition, dissensions, factions and envy; drunkenness, orgies, and the like. I warn you, as I did before, that those who live like this will not inherit the kingdom of God."

James 4:17 - "If anyone, then, knows the good they ought to do and doesn't do it, it is sin for them."

John 8:44 - "You belong to your father, the devil, and you want to carry out your father's desires. He was a murderer from the beginning, not holding to the truth, for there is no truth in him. When he lies, he speaks his native language, for he is a liar and the father of lies."

Romans 4:25 - "He was delivered over to death for our sins and was raised to life for our justification."

Ephesians 1:7-8 - "In him we have redemption through his blood, the forgiveness of sins, in accordance with the riches of God's grace [8] that he lavished on us. With all wisdom and understanding,"

1 Corinthians 15:57 - "But thanks be to God! He gives us the victory through our Lord Jesus Christ."

Romans 8:1 - "Therefore, there is now no condemnation for those who are in Christ Jesus,"

1 John 1:8-10 - "If we claim to be without sin, we deceive ourselves and the truth is not in us. If we confess our sins, he is faithful and just and will forgive us our sins and purify us from all unrighteousness. If we claim we have not sinned, we make him out to be a liar and his word is not in us."

1 John 1:9 - "If we confess our sins, he is faithful and just and will forgive us our sins and purify us from all unrighteousness."

James 5:16 - "Therefore confess your sins to each other and pray for each other so that you may be healed. The prayer of a righteous person is powerful and effective."

2 Corinthians 7:10 - "Godly sorrow brings repentance that leads to salvation and leaves no regret, but worldly sorrow brings death."

Luke 15:10 - "In the same way, I tell you, there is rejoicing in the presence of the angels of God over one sinner who repents."

Closing Prayer: Matthew 6:9-13

A FIRM FOUNDATION: Sin Q&A

Read and discuss each Bible passage with mentor. Write your answers in the space provided.

1. **According to 1 John 3:4, what is sin?**

2. **What examples of sin does Paul list in Galatians 5:19-21?**

3. **According to James 4:17, sin not only includes committing wrong, but what else?**

4. According to John 8:44, who is trying to lead you astray? How does this passage describe him and his tactics for temptation?

5. According to Romans 4:25, what did Jesus Christ do for our sins?

6. What does Jesus's death offer for the sins of all who believe in Him?

   a. Ephesians 1:7-8 - _____ of sins.

   b. 1 Corinthians 15:57 - _____ over sin and death.

   c. Romans 8:1 – No _____.

7. Read 1 John 1:8-10. Do believers still sin?   YES   NO

8. **What should we do when we sin?**

    a. 1 John 1:9 - Confess our sins to _____.

    b. James 5:16 – Confess our sins to _____.

    c. 2 Corinthians 7:10 - _____ of our sins.

9. **When you sin, how do you view God? What words would you use to describe Him?**

10. **Read Luke 15:10. How does God respond when we repent of our sins?**

CLOSING PRAYER: Matthew 6:9-13

MEMORY VERSE: Sin (Homework)

"For the wages of sin is death, but the gift of God is eternal life in Christ Jesus our Lord." Romans 6:23

You will also recite Ephesians 2:8-9 (Salvation: Weeks 1-2).

RENOVATION: Sin (Homework)

Reviewing the "Bad News" from "The Bridge Illustration," the Bible teaches:

1) All people have sinned and fall short of the glory of God (Rom. 3:23).
2) The wages of sin is death (Rom. 6:23).
3) There will be judgment after death (Hebr. 9:27).

Although sin may appear to offer short-term pleasure, excitement, or security, the Bible repeatedly illustrates the unavoidable hurt, pain, and sorrow that sin always produces. Hebrews 3:13 warns, "But encourage one another daily, as long as it is called 'Today,' so that none of you may be hardened by sin's deceitfulness." Left to ourselves, we will continue to be drawn to the false comfort, peace, and happiness offered by sin. The streets are littered with story after story of sin's broken promises and the inability of men and women to save themselves from themselves.

List 3 examples of how something/someone promised you life (pleasure, happiness, security), but ultimately led you to death (destruction or despair).

1.

2.

3.

No child grows up saying, "When I grow up, I want to be homeless." Life on the streets is no one's "dream come true," but oftentimes emerges as the result of a series of unexpected tragedies, a lack of support and guidance, reckless choices, addiction, and/or isolation.

List the major events and decisions responsible for your current situation.

How have your sinful actions robbed you of the life that God intends for you? What has sin painfully kept from you?

A well-known quote further illustrates the tangled webs we weave as slaves to sin, stating, "Sin will take you farther than you want to go, keep you longer than you want to stay, and cost you more than you want to pay." On our own, we are powerless to the downward spiral of sin. We think we can manage sin, but sin corrupts us, consumes us, and controls us. As Proverbs 6:27-28 cautions, "Can a man scoop fire into his lap without his clothes being burned? Can a man walk on hot coals without his feet being scorched?" We think we can play with fire, only for our pride to leave our lives in ashes.

Read and Reflect: "Then I acknowledged my sin to you and did not cover up my iniquity. I said, "I will confess my transgressions to the Lord." And you forgave the guilt of my sin." Psalms 32:5

"For as high as the heavens are above the earth, so great is his love for those who fear him; as far as the east is from the west, so far has he removed our transgressions from us." Psalms 103:11-13

"Whoever conceals their sins does not prosper, but the one who confesses and renounces them finds mercy." Proverbs 28:13

After completing the *Blueprint: Sin* lesson, how do you view your sin?

How do you view God?

What secret sin(s) or unconfessed sin(s) remain in your life? We encourage you to confess these sins to God (1 John 1:9) and share with them with your mentor (Jam. 5:16).

BLUEPRINT #3: SANCTIFICATION

RECITE:

Romans 6:23
Ephesians 2:8-9

REVIEW:

Renovation: Sin

God Transforms Homeless Hearts

Life on the streets, in a shelter, in a clinic, or in transitional housing can present overwhelming stress, suffering, and uncertainty. Between the trials that brought you here and the troubles that haunt you here, you might feel yourself slipping further and further away from not only where you want to be, but who you want to be… And, more importantly, who God calls you to be (2 Tim. 1:9).

The good news is that nothing is impossible for God (Matt. 19:26). No situation or struggle is too great for Him to overcome. In our trials, God's outstretched hand invites us to trust Him (2 Cor. 12:9-10). As we follow His Word and will for our lives, His truth transforms our hearts (Ps. 139:23-24, Rom. 12:1-2). Even if our circumstances on Earth do not improve, He can continue to restore us, renew us, and refine us (2 Cor. 4:16). With God, peace is always possible (Phil. 4:6-7).

Jesus Christ's death and resurrection remind us that even the worst suffering in the history of the world can be redeemed for good (1 Pet. 3:18). For many of you, rock bottom is the place where you finally began to admit and understand your need for God. Hopefully, your circumstances have humbled your heart to graciously give you an eye-opening view of the destruction caused by your sin, as well as a mind-blowing glimpse of your Savior's love, grace, and glory (Ps. 40). Throughout this lesson, you'll learn about God's blueprint for global and personal transformation through Jesus Christ.

Discuss: What is most challenging about your current circumstances?

GOD'S BLUEPRINT: A Summary of Sanctification

To sanctify means "to set apart and make holy." Jesus Christ paid the penalty for our sins on the cross. All true believers receive right standing, or peace with God (Rom. 5:1), through His perfect sacrifice and our perfect substitute, Jesus Christ (1 Pet. 3:18). Jesus paid the penalty we deserved for every sin we've committed-- past, present and future (2 Cor. 5:21). Though we were once dead in our sins, God graciously grants us new life through Christ (Eph. 2:4-5).

From the moment we believe until the moment we die, God calls us to become more and more like Christ (Rom. 8:29). This lifelong process of Christian growth is called sanctification. We are to love God and love others as He has perfectly loved us (1 John 4:19). In this life, progress is the goal. Perfection is unattainable because our sinful desires still exist, and continue to lead us astray, at times (2 Cor. 3:18). In the future, Christ will triumphantly return to remove Satan, sin, suffering, and death from the world (Rev. 21:4). He will perfect all believers (1 John 3:2). Christians refer to this final stage of renewal as glorification.

To better grasp this transformation process, consider a master sculptor. First, the sculptor purchases a marble slab. Next, he carefully chisels and chips away at the marble. During much of the sculpting process, the slab looks like a mess and the sculptor looks like a madman. Piece by piece, the artist's envisioned work of art emerges. In the end, the artist transforms the slab into a finished masterpiece, showcasing an astonishing level of skill, creativity, and brilliance.

Similarly, Christ paid our debt on the cross and repurposes us to participate in the holy mission of God (Eph. 2:10). We are to share His message of healing and hope in Christ, as we love and serve others (2 Cor. 5:14-21). In the future, God will showcase His finished masterpiece for all eternity, as Christ reigns over all believers in the new heaven and the new earth (Rev. 11:15). God is the perfect sculptor. Through faith, His Spirit continues to mold us be more and more like our perfect blueprint, Jesus Christ.

Discuss: In what areas do you least reflect Christ?

WEEK 5 BIBLE REFERENCES

Here are the passages we'll use during today's lesson:

Isaiah 55:8 - "For my thoughts are not your thoughts, neither are your ways my ways, declares the Lord."

Proverbs 28:26 - "Those who trust in themselves are fools, but those who walk in wisdom are kept safe.

Romans 12:2 - "Do not conform the pattern of this world, but be transformed by the renewing of your mind. Then you will be able to test and approve what God's will is—his good, pleasing, and perfect will.."

John 8:32 - "Then you will know the truth, and the truth will set you free."

Jeremiah 17:9 - "The heart is deceitful above all things, and beyond cure. Who can understand it?"

Mark 7:21-23 - "For it is from within, out of a person's heart, that evil thoughts come-- sexual immorality, theft, murder, adultery, greed, malice, deceit, lewdness, envy, slander, arrogance, and folly. All these evils come from inside and defile a person."

Psalm 51:10 - "Create in me a pure heart, O God, and renew a steadfast spirit within me."

Proverbs 3:5-6 - "Trust in the Lord with all your heart and lean not on your own understanding; in all your ways submit to him, and he will make your paths straight."

Galatians 5:19-21 - "The acts of the flesh are obvious: sexual immorality, impurity and debauchery; idolatry and witchcraft; hatred, discord, jealousy, fits of rage, selfish ambition, dissensions, factions and envy; drunkenness, orgies, and the like. I warn you, as I did before, that those who live like this will not inherit the kingdom of God."

John 15:5 - "I am the vine; you are the branches. If you remain in me and I in you, you will bear much fruit; apart from me you can do nothing."

Colossians 3:23-24 - "Whatever you do, work heartily, as for the Lord and not for men, knowing that from the Lord you will receive the inheritance as your reward. You are serving the Lord Christ."

Closing Prayer: 1 Thessalonians 5:23-24 - "May God himself, the God of peace, sanctify you through and through. May your whole spirit, soul and body be kept blameless at the coming of our Lord Jesus Christ. The one who calls you is faithful, and he will do it."

BUILDING BLOCKS: Head, Heart, Hands Model

The "Head, Heart, Hands Model" illustrates how our thoughts, affections, and lifestyle intersect, interact, and influence who we are and what we do. For example, when we feel angry, our anger clouds our judgment and prevents us from seeing the situation clearly. A distorted perspective and undeterred anger likely result in hurtful words or harmful actions. Like a skilled surgeon, the "Head, Heart, Hands Model" deploys the Word of God to diagnose us, deepen our relationship with God, and mend our damaged relationships with others.

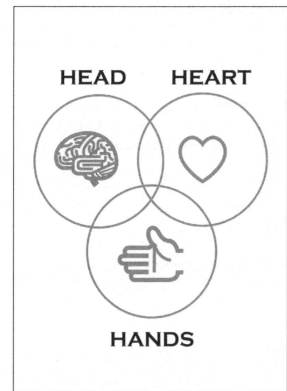

HEAD   **HEART**

HANDS

"Sanctify them by the truth; your word is truth." John 17:17

"Therefore, since we have these promises, dear friends, let us purify ourselves from everything that contaminates body and spirit, perfecting holiness out of reverence for God." 2 Corinthians 7:1

"As we gaze on Christ, the mind is informed, and the heart is inflamed, and the body begins to line up." Matt Chandler, The Village Church.

HEAD: The Truth Will Set You Free

The mind is a filing cabinet containing corrupt files and damaging lies. Our natural desires (the flesh) deceivingly direct us towards destructive decisions. God calls us to combat the corrupt files of the mind. His Word informs us and directs us towards His path of life, purpose, and peace, even in trials.

Diagnosis: Read Isaiah 55:8 and Proverbs 28:26.

Treatment: Read Romans 12:2 and John 8:32.

Discuss: How do these passages show the difference between God's wisdom and our own?

HEART: Follow God, not your Heart

The heart is a broken compass, leading us to seek our own desires and wants, rather than the freedom of God's will and way. We cannot save ourselves. We need God to save us from our sinful selves - from the misdirection of our deceitful heart. As pastor Todd Wagner claims, "God is not trying to rip us off, but set us free." Following His path offers unconditional love, life, joy, peace, and hope in all circumstances, as we trust Him to guide our lives.

Diagnosis: Read Jeremiah 17:9 and Mark 7:21-23.
Treatment: Read Psalm 51:10 and Proverbs 3:5-6.

Discuss: Do you agree that the "compass" of your heart is naturally broken? Why or why not?

HANDS: All Hands on Deck

The hands are our construction crew. With each day and decision, we choose to either serve God or serve ourselves. We can either follow His will for life and live according to His divine wisdom and power, or we can build our own frail kingdoms to satisfy our own selfish desires with our own feeble strength for own fleeting pleasure. The choice is ours. We can either feast on what is finite, or we can invest the time, treasure, and talents He has given us in His forever Kingdom.

Diagnosis: Read Galatians 5:19-21 and John 15:5.

Treatment: Read John 15:5 (again) and Colossians 3:23-24.

Discuss: What differences do these passages describe for those who build (live) according to God's plans rather than their own? Are you willing to surrender everything (relationships, values, habits, relationships, beliefs, etc.) to God's authority and guidance? Why or why not?

CLOSING PRAYER: 1 Thessalonians 5:23-24

MEMORY VERSE: Sanctification (Homework)

"I have been crucified with Christ and I no longer live, but Christ lives in me. The life I now live in the body, I live by faith in the Son of God, who loved me and gave himself for me." Galatians 2:20

You will also recite Ephesians 2:8-9 (Salvation: Weeks 1-2), and Romans 6:23 (Sin: Weeks 3-4).

INSPECTION: Sanctification (Homework)

Is "heart change" or "home change" more important to you? Explain your answer.

What influences (people, places, media, etc.) have most negatively affected how you see God, the world, and yourself?

What people or resources has God placed in your life to teach, encourage, or positively influence your faith?

Refer back to "The Head, Heart, Hands Model". List the changes you would like God to help accomplish in you.

    a. Head (Thinking)

    b. Heart (Emotions/Desires)

c. Hands (Actions)

How has God used your recent trials to grow your faith in Him?

BLUEPRINT #3: SANCTIFICATION

RECITE:

Galatians 2:20
Romans 6:23
Ephesians 2:8-9

REVIEW:

Inspection: Sanctification

WEEK 6 BIBLE REFERENCES

Here are the passages we'll use during today's lesson:

1 Thessalonians 4:3 - "It is God's will that you should be sanctified: that you should avoid sexual immorality;"

1 Peter 1:16 - "for it is written: 'Be holy, because I am holy.'"

John 3:16 - "For God so loved the world that he gave his one and only Son, that whoever believes in him shall not perish but have eternal life."

Romans 8:28-30 - "And we know that in all things God works for the good of those who love him, who have been called according to his purpose. For those God foreknew he also predestined to be conformed to the image of his Son, that he might be the firstborn among many brothers and sisters. And those he predestined, he also called; those he called, he also justified; those he justified, he also glorified."

1 John 3:2-3 - "Dear friends, now we are children of God, and what we will be has not yet been made known. But we know that when Christ appears, we shall be like him, for we shall see him as he is. All who have this hope in him purify themselves, just as he is pure."

John 14:26 - "But the Advocate, the Holy Spirit, whom the Father will send in my name, will teach you all things and will remind you of everything I have said to you."

1 Corinthians 6:19-20 - "Do you not know that your bodies are temples of the Holy Spirit, who is in you, whom you have received from God? You are not your own; you were bought at a price. Therefore honor God with your bodies."

1 Thessalonians 5:23-25 - "May God himself, the God of peace, sanctify you through and through. May your whole spirit, soul and body be kept blameless at the coming of our Lord Jesus Christ. The one who calls you is faithful, and he will do it. Brothers and sisters, pray for us."

1 Peter 1:3-9

Galatians 5:22-23 - "But the fruit of the Spirit is love, joy, peace, forbearance, kindness, goodness, faithfulness, gentleness and self-control. Against such things there is no law."

Closing Prayer: Psalm 139:33-37 - "Teach me, Lord, the way of your decrees, that I may follow it to the end. Give me understanding, so that I may keep your law and obey it with all my heart. Direct me in the path of your commands, for there I find delight. Turn my heart toward your statutes and not toward selfish gain. Turn my eyes away from worthless things; preserve my life according to your word."

A FIRM FOUNDATION: Sanctification Q&A

Read and discuss each Bible passage with mentor. Write your answers in the space provided.

1. **Read 1 Thessalonians 4:3. Sanctification is the _____ of**

    God.

2. **Read 1 Peter 1:16. God commands us to "Be _____**

   because _____ am _____."

3. **The Will of God for the Believer**

   a. **Justification:** Read John 3:16. It is God's will to give

      eternal life to all who _____ in Jesus Christ.

   b. **Sanctification:** Read Romans 8:28-30. It is God's will to

      conform all believers to the image of_____.

   c. **Glorification:** Read 1 John 3:2-3. It is God's will that we

      become like Christ when Christ_____.

4. **John 14:26 describes the Holy Spirit as "the Helper (NASB)." God's blueprint for change is only possible through the power of the Holy Spirit working in God's people.**

   a. According to 1 Corinthians 6:19-20, how does this passage refer to our bodies? In light of this truth, how should we live?

   b. According to 1 Thessalonians 5:23-25, what does this passage say to those who believe, "People can't change… ?"

5. **Read 1 Peter 1:3-9. What does God offer to all believers?**

   a. Verse 3 –

   b. Verse 4 –

   c. Verse 5 –

d. Verses 6-7 –

e. Verses 8-9 -

6. **Read Galatians 5:22-23. What "fruit" does the Holy Spirit bear in believers, as He transforms them?**

CLOSING PRAYER: Psalm 119:33-37

MEMORY VERSE – Sanctification (Homework)

"I have been crucified with Christ and I no longer live, but Christ lives in me. The life I now live in the body, I live by faith in the Son of God, who loved me and gave himself for me." Galatians 2:20

You will also recite Ephesians 2:8-9 (Salvation: Weeks 1-2) and Romans 6:23 (Sin: Weeks 3-4).

RENOVATION: Sanctification (Homework)

The Bible presents a cohesive story of God's activity past, present, and future. Many teachers have broken the Bible down into four major eras: Creation, Fall, Redemption, and Restoration. Hopefully, this summary will help you more effectively read, understand, apply, and teach the Bible to others.

1. **Creation:** First, God graciously created and brought order to the entire universe. His creation functioned and flourished exactly how He intended and He declared it "good." The pinnacle of creation was man and woman, who were created in the image of God. He made humans different from all other creatures– unique souls possessing dignity and worth, the ability to reason, the capacity for relationship, and the responsibility to

reflect God and rule over creation as His representatives on Earth.

2. **Fall:** Next, sin entered the world through the disobedience of man. Adam and Eve fell prey to the Devil's deception by eating the fruit of the tree of the knowledge of good and evil. This act of rebellion caused everything and everyone to fall under the tragic curse and corruption of sin.

3. **Redemption:** A little more than 2,000 years ago, just as God promised, He sent His Son Jesus Christ to restore fellowship between God and fallen humanity. Jesus was fully God and fully man. He lived a perfect life, suffered and died on the cross for our sins, and resurrected from the dead. Through faith, all who believe in Him are forgiven and adopted into God's forever family. After Christ ascended to heaven, the Holy Spirit was sent to Earth to start, strengthen, and sustain the Church, in anticipation of Christ's 2nd coming.

4. **Restoration:** Someday, Jesus will return to judge and rule the world. In the end, He will triumphantly remove sin, suffering, and death from the world, once and for all. He will restore the universe and resurrect all believers to live out God's perfect blueprint. With Christ as King, everything will function and flourish for eternity exactly how God has always intended.

It is not about inviting God into our stories, but Him inviting us into His. Ultimately, nothing has stood in the way of God's will from coming true and nothing will!

In light of Christ's past sacrifice and His future return, how will you live differently in the present?

Hebrews 6:19 refers to the believer's hope in Christ, "as an anchor for the soul, firm and secure." When you experience the "storms of life," where do you place your hope and why?

As promised in Revelation 21:5, Christ will one day return to make all things new. He will transform both you and your circumstances. This future reality offers you a peace that poverty cannot rob from you, a hope that homelessness cannot extinguish, a strength that sin and Satan cannot stop, and a life that death cannot devour.

In Philippians 4:12-13, Paul exalts Christ as the key to contentment and endurance in any and all circumstances. After experiencing trial after trial, Paul testifies, "I have learned the secret of being content in any and every situation, whether well fed or hungry, whether living in plenty or in want. I can do all this through him who gives me strength."

What attitudes or actions do you most desire God to change in you, in order to better endure your circumstances?

Of the 12 struggles listed below, which 3 struggles most relate to your current situation?

JESUS CHRIST: God's Blueprint for Change

Weary? Christ offers rest. (Matt. 11:28)

Worried? Christ offers peace. (Col. 3:15)

Weak? Christ is powerful. (2 Cor. 12:9)

Wounded? Christ is our healer. (Luke 5:31-32)

Lost? Christ is the Way. (John 14:6)

Lonely? Christ is our brother and friend. (Mark 3:35, John 15:15)

Confused? Christ is the Truth. (John 8:32)

Hopeless? Christ is the Life. (John 14:6)

Helpless? Christ is the Mighty One. (Is. 60:16)

Homeless? Christ is preparing a forever place for you. (John 14:3)

Hungry? Christ is our Living Bread. (John 6:35)

Suffering? Christ is our Savior. (Luke 2:11)

Look up the corresponding verses to each struggle you listed. In your own words, what comfort does the truth of these passages offer to you in your current trials?

BLUEPRINT #4: SUBMISSION

RECITE:

Galatians 2:20
Romans 6:23
Ephesians 2:8-9

REVIEW:

Renovation: Sanctification

Submission, Even on the Streets

Waking up each morning to the problems and pains of your present situation may seem overwhelming. You may feel alone. You may feel like a leaky boat lost at sea. Your sails have been ravaged and the storm rages on all around you. You may feel like you are taking on more water each day. It may seem like as soon as you stick your finger in one hole to plug the leak, another hole emerges. And another. And another. As the water rises, all hope appears lost.

Sound familiar? The humbling truth is that you cannot save yourself (Rom. 3:10-12). In this broken world, you cannot bear your burdens alone. You are in desperate need of help. As you may have heard in other recovery programs, the first step towards healing and getting the help you need is to admit your inability to save yourself or sustain yourself (John 15:5).

Fortunately, God is a God of rescue and restoration (Col. 1:13-14). Nothing is impossible for Him (Matt. 19:26). He freely offers you everything you need to persevere through every trial and trouble (2 Pet. 1:3). You are not alone. God has not forgotten you or forsaken you. He loves you and nothing can separate you from His love (Rom. 8:37-39).

He hears the prayers of His people (1 John 5:14) and can help you endure today's trials (1 Cor. 10:13).

However, accepting the help God offers may be difficult. His help may not come on your terms and timing, but His Word, will, and all of His ways are perfect (Ps. 18:30). To submit to God is to recognize and revere Him alone as God (Matt. 6:33). The Bible promises you can trust that He knows what is best for you (Is. 55:8-9), wants what is best for you (John 10:10), and is actively accomplishing what is best for you (Rom. 8:28). As difficult it may seem, submission to God is always the answer in your time of need.

Graciously, God also offers you the help of His people. All Christians are a part of the family of God, intended to be His support system on earth (Rom. 12:5). Though far from perfect, the Church should serve on the frontlines of helping the lost and lonely through prayer, discipleship, counsel, community, guidance, and provision (Gal. 6:9-10).

Often, financial and physical support may come with a cost. Your church may ask you to take specific steps to ensure their help is for your long-term good and protection (Heb. 13:17). True help does not enable you, but educates you and empowers you as a "hand-up," instead of a handout (Eph. 4:28). As believers, we are all called to not only submit to God, but also to His appointed leaders in the Church (Heb. 13:17).

Lastly, God provides help in the form of national and local government agencies and organizations. In a broken world, these systems are imperfect and can present additional opportunities for setbacks, stress, and frustration. However, you will likely need their help. To move forward, you will have to play by the rules. If you treat the employees you meet with respect, kindness, patience, and humility, they will be much more likely to help you (Rom. 13:7). If you are proactive, on time, and respect their guidelines, everything can go much more smoothly. Ultimately, God calls each of us to submit to the government authorities and the laws in place, in order to help us, not hurt us (Rom. 13:1).

Discuss: What positive and negative experiences have you had with Christians or being a part of a church?

GOD'S BLUEPRINT: *A Summary of Submission*

What words come to mind when you hear the word "submission?" For most people, the thought of submission of any kind makes them squirm in their seat, or raise their voice in anger or objection. In wrestling or mixed martial arts, fighters "submit" when the painful hold inflicted by their opponent forces them to "tap out" and admit defeat. For many of us, our feelings toward submission have been significantly influenced by negative experiences with government authorities, the police, teachers, or family. As strange as it sounds, the Bible teaches surrender as the key to victory (Acts 2:21). Through faith, the strength of God is unleashed in you through your humble submission to Him (2 Cor. 12:9), as perfectly modeled through Christ's life, death, and resurrection.

Imagine life as a car. Biblical submission is not thinking, "Man, God sure is a great driver," or even shouting such a phrase. Christian submission means giving God the keys to lead your life and direct your desires and decisions (Rom. 8:12-13). Giving complete control to God is not easy, since our desires and plans oftentimes conflict with His. You may be asking yourself, "Why should I let God do all the driving? Can I really trust Him?"

Submission to God is not without good reason! First, He created everything in existence, including you and me (Col. 1:16). Since He designed us, He knows not only the right destination for us, but also the right route for us to take to get there. He is not only the perfect driver, but also the perfect mechanic (Ps. 18:30). He intimately knows every part of us. He knows our lives, our hearts, our hurts, and our minds (Ps. 139:1-4). He knows everything we have ever thought, said, or done, and still He loves us. He sent His Son to rescue us from our sinful selves. Christ's suffering and sacrificial death forever prove we can completely trust God with every mile He has lovingly mapped out for our lives (Rom. 5:8, Eph. 2:10). If He is perfect and powerful enough to be our Savior, He is certainly perfect and powerful enough to be the Lord of our lives each day.

As our pastor often reminds us, "God is not trying to rip us off, but set us free (John 8:32)." He is a good Father, who only gives good gifts to

His children (Jam. 1:17). In His hands, even suffering can be a good gift to grow us and glorify Him. He is not trying to tempt us, trick us, or trap us. Rather, He invites us into a deep relationship with Him, in order for us to experience life, love, hope, healing, value, and purpose beyond anything we ever could have experienced on our own (John 10:10).

In the end, following Christ is never easy (Luke 9:23). As Jesus warned His disciples, dying to ourselves is the "not-so-secret secret" to truly finding life (Matt. 16:25). Even when we obey God, we will still face suffering (John 16:33). Fortunately, God always grants a way out to endure temptation (1 Cor. 10:13). Trusting God can be tough, but trusting Him is always for our best (Rom. 8:35-37). Truly, Christ plus nothing equals everything (Eph. 1:4).

Discuss: What keeps you from trusting God with all of your heart and life?

WEEK 7 BIBLE REFERENCES

Here are the passages we'll use during today's lesson:

Galatians 5:16-17 - "So I say, walk by the Spirit, and you will not gratify the desires of the flesh. For the flesh desires what is contrary to the Spirit, and the Spirit what is contrary to the flesh. They are in conflict with each other, so that you are not to do whatever you want."

Romans 8:5-8 - "Those who live according to the flesh have their minds set on what the flesh desires; but those who live in accordance with the Spirit have their minds set on what the Spirit desires. The mind governed by the flesh is death, but the mind governed by the Spirit is life and peace. The mind governed by the flesh is hostile to God; it does not submit to God's law, nor can it do so. Those who are in the realm of the flesh cannot please God."

Closing Prayer: Matthew 6:9-13 - "This, then, is how you should pray: Our Father in heaven, hallowed be your name, your kingdom come, your will be done, on earth as it is in heaven. Give us today our daily bread. And forgive us our debts, as we also have forgiven our debtors. And lead us not into temptation, but deliver us from the evil one. Amen."

BUILDING BLOCKS: " Thy Way, My Way Model"

The Bible teaches the drastic contrast between following our natural, sinful desires and following God. Left to ourselves, our decisions will leave us destined for spiritual suicide and likely physical destruction. As believers, God offers a whole new road to travel-- one guided by His purpose, power, and perspective. The "Thy Way, My Way Model" illustrates the differences between following our fallen flesh and following our holy, perfect God.

Read through the figure below, as well as Galatians 5:16-17 and Romans 8:5-8.

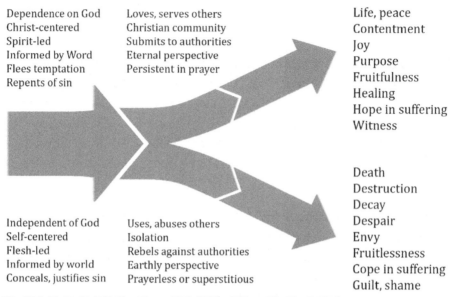

THY WILL BE DONE

Dependence on God	Loves, serves others	Life, peace
Christ-centered	Christian community	Contentment
Spirit-led	Submits to authorities	Joy
Informed by Word	Eternal perspective	Purpose
Flees temptation	Persistent in prayer	Fruitfulness
Repents of sin		Healing
		Hope in suffering
		Witness

		Death
		Destruction
		Decay
Independent of God	Uses, abuses others	Despair
Self-centered	Isolation	Envy
Flesh-led	Rebels against authorities	Fruitlessness
Informed by world	Earthly perspective	Cope in suffering
Conceals, justifies sin	Prayerless or superstitious	Guilt, shame

MY WILL BE DONE

Discuss: What have you learned about the differences between following God's will and your will? Are you willing to completely submit your life to God and allow His will to be done in your life?

CLOSING PRAYER: Matthew 6:9-13

MEMORY VERSE: Submission (Homework)

"Trust in the Lord with all your heart and lean not on your own understanding; in all your ways submit to him, and he will make your paths straight." Proverbs 3:5-6

You will also recite Ephesians 2:8-9 (Salvation: Weeks 1-2), Romans 6:23 (Sin: Weeks 3-4), and Galatians 2:20 (Sanctification: Weeks 5-6).

INSPECTION: *Submission (Homework)*

How would you describe your life when God is not in the driver seat?

When did rebellion against God hurt you the most?

When did submission to God bless you the most?

Besides God, what other authorities have you failed to properly submit to in life, and how? Read each corresponding passage and fill out the table below.

AUTHORITY	CONFLICT HISTORY In what ways have you not submitted?
Government/Police Romans 13:1-2	
Church Hebrews 13:17	
Parents/Spouse Ephesians 5:21-6:3	
Work Ephesians 6:5-8	

Week 8

BLUEPRINT #4: SUBMISSION

RECITE:

Proverbs 3:5-6
Galatians 2:20
Romans 6:23
Ephesians 2:8-9

REVIEW:

Inspection: Submission

Week 8 Bible References

Here are the passages we'll use during today's lesson:

Psalm 18:2 - "The Lord is my rock, my fortress and my deliverer; my God is my rock, in whom I take refuge, my shield and the horn of my salvation, my stronghold."

Psalm 18:30 - "As for God, his way is perfect: The Lord's word is flawless; he shields all who take refuge in him."

Psalm 23:1-2 - "The Lord is my shepherd, I lack nothing. He makes me lie down in green pastures, he leads me beside quiet waters, he refreshes my soul."

Psalm 89:11 - "The heavens are yours, and yours also the earth; you founded the world and all that is in it."

Psalm 136:1 - "Give thanks to the Lord, for he is good; His love endures forever."

Psalm 139:4 - "Before a word is on my tongue you, Lord, know it completely."

Proverbs 3:5-6 - "Trust in the Lord with all your heart and lean not on your own understanding; in all your ways submit to him, and he will make your paths straight."

John 6:38 - "For I have come down from heaven not to do my will but to do the will of him who sent me."

Mark 10:45 - "For even the Son of Man did not come to be served, but to serve, and to give his life as a ransom for many."

Luke 19:10 - "For the Son of Man came to seek and to save the lost."

Matthew 4:4 - " Jesus answered, "It is written: 'Man shall not live on bread alone, but on every word that comes from the mouth of God.'"

Hebrews 9:14 - "How much more, then, will the blood of Christ, who through the eternal Spirit offered himself unblemished to God, cleanse our consciences from acts that lead to death, so that we may serve the living God!"

1 Corinthians 6:19-20 - "Do you not know that your bodies are temples of the Holy Spirit, who is in you, whom you have received from God? You are not your own; [20] you were bought at a price. Therefore honor God with your bodies."

Matthew 6:24 - "No one can serve two masters. Either you will hate the one and love the other, or you will be devoted to the one and despise the other. You cannot serve both God and money."

1 Peter 4:10 - "Each of you should use whatever gift you have received to serve others, as faithful stewards of God's grace in its various forms. If anyone speaks, they should do so as one who speaks the very words of God."

Ephesians 4:15-16 – "Instead, speaking the truth in love, we will grow to become in every respect the mature body of him who is the head, that is, Christ. From him the whole body, joined and held together by every supporting ligament, grows and builds itself up in love, as each part does its work."

Closing Prayer: Psalm 84:10-12 – "Better is one day in your courts than a thousand elsewhere; I would rather be a doorkeeper in the house of my God than dwell in the tents of the wicked. For the LORD God is a sun and shield; the LORD bestows favor and honor; no good thing does he withhold from those whose walk is blameless. LORD Almighty, blessed is the one who trusts in you."

A FIRM FOUNDATION: Submission Q&A

Read and discuss each Bible passage with mentor. Write your answers in the space provided.

1. **The goal of the Christian life is to know God, love God, and follow God. For each passage, list the reason we have to submit to God.**

KNOW GOD, LOVE GOD, FOLLOW GOD	
Psalm 18:2	
Psalm 18:30	
Psalm 23:1-2	
Psalm 89:11	
Psalm 136:1	
Psalm 139:4	

2. **How does the Bible teach submission to God as a blessing to us in Proverbs 3:5-6?**

    a. Command:

    b. Benefit:

3. **"Model Submission: Jesus Christ" – In the following passages, you will see God's blueprint for submission, as perfectly modeled by Jesus Christ. Through His sinless life, death, and resurrection, He accomplished what we cannot. Through faith, God allows us to grow in Christ-likeness, regardless of our circumstances.**

    a. Read John 6:38: What was Jesus's mindset?

    b. Read Mark 10:45: What was Jesus's mission?

    c. Read Luke 19:10: Who was Jesus's mission field?

    d. Read Matthew 4:4: What was Jesus's manual?

    e. Read Hebrews 9:14: Who empowered Jesus?

4. Colossians 3:17 declares, "And whatever you do, whether in word or deed, do it all in the name of the Lord Jesus...," meaning God calls us to complete submission, including:

    a. 1 Corinthians 6:19-20 – Our _____.

    b. Matthew 6:24 – Our _____.

    c. 1 Peter 4:10 – Our _____.

5. The Bible refers to the Church as the body of Christ, as well as the bride of Christ. Christians are not to live in isolation, but in unity and harmony with their fellow believers under the authority and guidance of church leadership. Read Ephesians 4:15-16 and Hebrews 10:24-25.

   Discuss some of the blessings God intends for you to experience through church membership and participation.

6. Are you a current member of a healthy Bible-teaching, Christ-centered local church?

                 YES   NO

7. If not, are you willing to submit to God's blueprint for church membership? Why or why not?

CLOSING PRAYER: Psalm 84:10-12

MEMORY VERSE: Submission (Homework)

"Trust in the Lord with all your heart and lean not on your own understanding; in all your ways submit to him, and he will make your paths straight." Proverbs 3:5-6

You will also recite Ephesians 2:8-9 (Salvation: Weeks 1-2), Romans 6:23 (Sin: Weeks 3-4), and Galatians 2:20 (Sanctification: Weeks 5-6).

RENOVATION: Submission (Homework)

Admittedly, submission to God is not easy, especially on the streets or in a shelter. Temptation lies around every corner. Suffering, sorrow, and stress greet you each morning. Nothing is simple. Your to-do-list continues to grow and grow. Agencies may seem ineffective or inefficient. Support seems slim and hope seems dim.

You may think, "I'll do it myself. I'll do it my way. If I break the rules just this once, no one will know." Or, maybe you are past the point of caring and now think to yourself, "I give up. What's the point? It is what is." Please don't give up. With God's help, there is always hope.

Every decision, every day you have the choice to trust and obey God. Either you can rely on His plan, power, and provision for your life, or you can choose to follow your own path and preferences, hindered by your own shortcomings, struggles, and weaknesses.

What presents the greatest barriers to following God?

Even on the streets, you must consider, are you living the Christ-centered life or the self-centered life? In Matthew 6:33, Jesus commands, "But seek first his kingdom and his righteousness, and all these things will be given to you as well. " When your relationship with Him is your top priority, real change happens. When you pursue and practice the wisdom of God's Word (alongside fellow believers) you can make informed decisions, establish wise priorities, and guard against temptation, the devil, and other negative influences.

List *your top 7 actual priorities*, starting with the most important.

What do your life, actions, and thoughts reveal as most important to you? Be honest.

Possible Examples:

Family, Friends, House, Sports, Drugs, Sex, Money, God, Job, Church, Health, Hobbies, Relationship

1.

2.

3.

4.

5.

6.

7.

List what you believe *your top 7 priorities should be*, based upon what you have learned through *Blueprint* and your previous study.

1.

2.

3.

4.

5.

6.

7.

How different are the two lists? How could living out the 2nd list positively affect your current circumstances?

Submission to God emerges as sole source of true spiritual blessing. Obedience to His path and reliance on His promises, power, and provision will transform your heart, as you endure life's trials and take practical steps forward. While it is possible to make physical, professional, and financial progress on your own, Psalm 127:1 warns against the futility of not seeking God's guidance, support, and strength, "Unless the LORD builds the house, the builders labor in vain." You will not become the man or woman that God intends without His help. You cannot live out the will of God without following the Word of God.

BLUEPRINT #5: SPIRITUAL DISCIPLINES

RECITE:

Proverbs 3:5-6
Galatians 2:20
Romans 6:23
Ephesians 2:8-9

REVIEW:

Renovation: Submission

Holiness in Homelessness

The Scriptures remind us, "A man reaps what he sows (Gal 6:7)." As you have experienced, life operates according to this principle of cause and effect. Choices have consequences. In your current circumstances, it is as critical as ever to remain dependent on God, seek the support of other Christians, make disciplined decisions, and form healthy habits. If you do not His instruction, a lack of discipline will lead to further destruction and greater despair (Prov. 5:23).

Throughout your life, you have developed habits for how you think, speak, and act. Your experience, education, environment, parents, peers, and genes may influence your perspective and practices. Many of your habits formed long ago and have been performed for years, making change difficult. You may live the only way you know how. However, just because you have been doing something your whole life does not make it right.

Humility is the first step towards change (1 Pet. 5:6). Face the facts. You do not have all the answers. Your situation, speech, thoughts, and actions reflect this truth. None of us do. Sadly, some unhealthy habits in your life may have turned into full-blown addictions. Addictions can cause you to continue to make the same harmful decisions, even though they have repeatedly devastated your life and relationships along the way (Tit. 3:3).

Fortunately, our God is a God of rescue, resurrection, and radical transformation. He has the power to raise the dead to life, heal addicts, purify prostitutes, and set slaves to sin free. No habit is too powerful for Him to overcome, although you will not find complete freedom from temptation or suffering in this life. However, through Christ, change and freedom are always possible (John 11:25, Rom. 6:1-14). In Him, we are new creations (2 Cor. 5:17). We have been given God's Word, Spirit, and people to help us follow Him. Through His Word, God reveals to us the true account of who He is, who we are, and how we should live in light of His perfect holiness, faithfulness, and mercy.

Remember, following God does not mean your life will be pain-free, or trouble-free, as Christ's life, death, and teachings revealed (John 16:33). As we follow Him, God transforms us to be more like Him. We can trust Him at all times. In the words of pastor Charles Stanley, "Obey God and leave the consequences to Him." Obedience looks like learning God's Word, living out God's Word, and sharing His Word (Ez. 7:10). As you faithfully follow Him, God will bear fruit in you for your own good and the good of others (John 15:5).

In whatever you face today, the God of the heavens and the earth hears you. He desires to speak to you through His Word because He cares deeply for you (Ps. 145:18-19). He wants to lead you to true life and His perfect love (John 10:10). As you humble yourself before God, He will lift you up in His perfect timing and way (1 Pet. 5:6).

*For many physical, mental, and emotional struggles, professional help may be advised as a compliment to the care provided through prayer, discipleship, and church support.

Discuss: What habits or attitudes most hinder your relationship with God and relationships with others? Do you believe healing, growth, and change are possible?

GOD'S BLUEPRINT: A Summary of Spiritual Disciplines

Discipline is defined as "training expected to produce a specific character or pattern of behavior." Consider a world-class athlete. To achieve peak-performance, the athlete follows a strict regimen of intense training, careful nutrition, and intentional rest and recovery. An coach monitors the athlete and makes adjustments to enhance his performance along the way. Success cannot come without sacrifice. The athlete willingly gives up any hindrances towards attaining his established goals.

Just like an athlete, certain habits can either help or harm our faithfulness and fruitfulness as Christians. With spiritual disciplines, practice does not make perfect. Rather, Bible study and prayer connect us to the God who is perfect and whose Word is perfect. These practices can connect us to Him, as we grow in knowledge and love of Him. Proper prayer and study also inspire love for others (Matt. 22:37). Although the Holy Spirit is the One who changes us, these habits provide fertile soil for godly growth to occur (John 15:5-8). While the Bible recommends a variety of important spiritual disciplines, such as evangelism, giving, service, and fasting, we will primarily focus our teaching on Bible study and prayer.

First, the Bible is unlike any other book on the planet, because God produced it (2 Tim. 3:16-17) and preserves it (Matt. 24:35). Therefore, the Bible is perfect and powerful (Ps. 18:30). The Bible is alive and active (Heb. 4:12) and able to transform our hearts, minds, and lives (John 17:17) to be more like Christ. To understand and apply the Word of God, we need the help of the Spirit of God (1 Cor. 2:12). Ultimately, God intends the Bible to fuel our affections for Him (Ps. 119). How amazing it is that He has spoken to us to reveal truths about His perfect nature, our fallen nature, and His perfect plan of redemption and restoration through Jesus Christ!

As Christians, we are to live as "people of the Book" in all we do. As James commands, "Do not merely listen to the Word, and so deceive ourselves, but do what it says (Jam. 1:22)." By following His Word, we live out His will (Rom. 12:2). Since God offers such an amazing tool to teach us, encourage us, and empower us, reading and applying His Word must remain a daily priority throughout our lifetime (Josh. 1:8).

If personal Bible study is new to you, getting started may seem intimidating. A great next step is to join a Bible study group with leaders and other believers who can teach you. Otherwise, try starting with one of the Gospels (Matthew, Mark, Luke, or John) or Psalms.

Other great Bible study resources:

- Jointhejourney.com – Watermark Community Church's online Bible Study.
- Thebibleproject.com – Animated videos for every book of the Bible and numerous biblical topics.
- Gotquestions.com – Answers to thousands of questions about the Bible and issues of life and faith.
- Blueletterbible.org – A comprehensive source of Bible study tools and resources.
- Navigators.org – An online resource library for discipleship.

As Bible study can increase our understanding, obedience, and worship, prayer can also deepen our relationship with God. Prayer is talking with God. Just as in any relationship, communication is essential for connection (Ps. 145:18). God calls us to pray constantly (1 Thess. 5:17). Through prayer, we can share everything on our hearts and minds with Him (1 Pet. 5:7). God invites us to praise and thank Him (1 Thess. 5:16-18), petition Him for changes we desire for others and ourselves (Phil. 4:6-7), confess our sins to Him (1 John 1:9), and share our feelings and fears with Him (Heb. 4:16). It is important to note that God is not a genie who bows to our wishes. Rather, we are to bow our hearts to Him in worship. Prayer reminds us that He is God and we are not. As we pray to Him, we are to yield to His perfect plan, purpose, and power (John 15:16).

Discuss: Why are Bible study and prayer essential to your daily life? What keeps you from being a more disciplined and committed follower of Christ?

WEEK 9 BIBLE REFERENCES

Our passages are lengthier reads this week. Therefore, you will need to look up the following Psalms:

Psalm 8

Psalm 51:10-17

Psalm 100

Psalm 13

Closing Prayer - Psalm 119:33-37

BUILDING BLOCKS: The "A.C.T.S. Prayer Model"

The Bible models many methods and purposes for prayer. A common acronym used to teach four common types of prayer is the "A.C.T.S. Prayer Model." Read the description of each prayer type below, as well as the corresponding sample passage.

THE "A.C.T.S. PRAYER MODEL"		
Adoration	Praise God for who He is and what He's done.	**Example: Psalm 8**
Confession	Admit sins to God.	**Example: Psalm 51:10-17**
Thanksgiving	Thank God for who He is and what He's done.	**Example: Psalm 100**
Supplication	Ask God to help you or others.	**Example: Psalm 13**

Discuss:

1) How often do you pray? When do you pray?
2) What type of prayer do you pray most often? Least often?
3) Do you only pray for yourself? Do you only pray by yourself?
4) Do you use God's Word to help you pray?

Mentors, what would you suggest for a more Christ-centered, God-honoring prayer life?

CLOSING PRAYER: Psalm 119:33-37

MEMORY VERSE: Spiritual Disciplines (Homework)

"Your word is a lamp for my feet, a light on my path." Psalm 119:105

You will also recite Ephesians 2:8-9 (Salvation: Weeks 1-2), Romans 6:23 (Sin: Weeks 3-4), Galatians 2:20 (Sanctification: Weeks 5-6), and Proverbs 3:5-6 (Submission: Weeks 7-8).

INSPECTION: Spiritual Disciplines (Homework)

How often do you read the Bible? Daily, occasionally, never?

What are some reasons to study the Bible each day?

On a scale of 1-10 (10 = daily) , how often do you...

    a. Ask God to change your circumstances/health: _____.

    b. Ask God to change your character/faith: _____.

    c. Ask God to help others: _____.

    d. Ask God for wisdom and understanding: _____.

    e. Ask God to save/bless your enemies: _____.

    f. Ask for God's will to be done: _____.

    g. Praise God for who He is and what He's done: _____.

    h. Thank God for what He's done: _____.

    i. Confess your sin: _____.

Based upon all you have read and learned throughout this lesson, what changes should you make to your prayer life?

Fill in the blank spaces of the "A.C.T.S." prayer chart with your own personal list of praises to God, confessions to God, thanks to God, and requests to God.

YOUR PERSONAL "A.C.T.S." PRAYER CHART		
Adoration	Praise God for who He is and what He's done.	
Confession	Admit sins to God.	
Thanksgiving	Thank God for who He is and what He's done.	
Supplication	Ask God to help you or others.	

BLUEPRINT #5: SPIRITUAL DISCIPLINES

RECITE:

Psalm 119:105
Proverbs 3:5-6
Galatians 2:20
Romans 6:23
Ephesians 2:8-9

REVIEW:

Inspection: Spiritual Disciplines

Week 10 Bible References

Here are the passages we'll use during today's lesson:

1 Timothy 4:7 - "Have nothing to do with godless myths and old wives' tales; rather, train yourself to be godly."

2 Timothy 3:16-17 - "All Scripture is God-breathed and is useful for teaching, rebuking, correcting and training in righteousness, so that the servant of God may be thoroughly equipped for every good work."

James 3:13-18 – "Who is wise and understanding among you? Let them show it by their good life, by deeds done in the humility that comes from wisdom. But if you harbor bitter envy and selfish ambition in your hearts, do not boast about it or deny the truth. Such "wisdom" does not come down from heaven but is earthly, unspiritual, demonic. For where you have envy and selfish ambition, there you find disorder and every evil practice. But the wisdom that comes from heaven is first of all pure; then peace-loving, considerate, submissive, full of mercy and good fruit, impartial and sincere. Peacemakers who sow in peace reap a harvest of righteousness."

Psalm 1-"Blessed is the man who walks not in the counsel of the wicked, nor stands in the way of sinners, nor sits in the seat of scoffers; but his delight is in the law of the Lord, and on his law he meditates day and night. He is like a tree planted by streams of water that yields its fruit in its season, and its leaf does not wither. In all that he does, he prospers. The wicked are not so, but are like chaff that the wind drives away. Therefore the wicked will not stand in the judgment, nor sinners in the congregation of the righteous; for the Lord knows the way of the righteous, but the way of the wicked will perish."

James 1:22 - "Do not merely listen to the word, and so deceive yourselves. Do what it says."

Psalm 119:9-11 - "How can a young person stay on the path of purity? By living according to your word. I seek you with all my heart; do not let me stray from your commands. I have hidden your word in my heart that I might not sin against you."

Romans 8:26-27 - " In the same way, the Spirit helps us in our weakness. We do not know what we ought to pray for, but the Spirit himself intercedes for us through wordless groans. And he who searches our hearts knows the mind of the Spirit, because the Spirit intercedes for God's people in accordance with the will of God."

1 Thessalonians 5:16-18 - "Rejoice always, pray continually, give thanks in all circumstances; for this is God's will for you in Christ Jesus."

James 4:3 - "When you ask, you do not receive, because you ask with wrong motives, that you may spend what you get on your pleasures."

A FIRM FOUNDATION: *Spiritual Disciplines Q&A*

Read and discuss each Bible passage with mentor. Write your answers in the space provided.

1. **Read 1 Timothy 4:7. What is a primary goal of practicing spiritual disciplines?**

2. **Read 2 Timothy 3:16-17 to answer the following questions.**

    a. Who is the ultimate source of all Scripture?

    b. List the 4 ways the passage calls us to apply the Scriptures.

    c. What do the Scriptures ultimately prepare you for in life?

3. **Read James 3:13-18. What is the difference between earthly wisdom and godly wisdom?**

    a. Earthly wisdom (v. 14-16):

b. Godly wisdom (v. 13, 17-18):

4. **Read Psalm 1. What benefits does walking according to God's Word offer?**

5. **Read James 1:22. What type of Bible study does James warn against?**

6. **Read Psalm 119:9-11. How is Scripture memory beneficial?**

7. **Read Romans 8:26-27. Who helps us pray according to God's will? What comfort does this give you?**

8. **Read 1 Thessalonians 5:16-18. What is God's will for our prayer life?**

9. **Read James 4:3. What warning does James offer regarding prayer?**

CLOSING PRAYER

As guided by your previous answers, spend time in prayer with your mentor.

RENOVATION: Spiritual Disciplines (Homework)

Even in homelessness, holiness remains a primary goal for the Christian life (Rom. 6:19, 2 Cor. 7:1, Eph. 4:22-24). Neither your difficult circumstances or the unending grace of God give you an excuse to sin (Rom. 6:15-23). A lack of discipline, support, structure, and responsibility can all contribute to further godlessness on the streets, as old habits worsen and new unhealthy habits form (Prov. 5:23, Prov. 18:1, Jam. 4:17).

2 Peter 1:4-11 describe the undisciplined as spiritually ineffective, unproductive, near-sighted, and blind. When you stray from God's Word and will, you will continue to stumble and follow your sinful desires towards destruction. If this has been your story in the past, change is still possible. As Psalm 19:7 testifies, "The instructions of the LORD are perfect, reviving the soul (NLT)." You don't have to continue to be your own worst enemy. His Word offers a better way. He can redeem your struggles and repurpose you for your own good, the good of others, and His glory.

Regular prayer and devotion to His Word allow for the possibility of growth, gratitude, and hope in all circumstances. A deeper relationship with God is what will bless you the most in life, but closeness does not just happen with time or age. Just like with a friend or family member, developing a relationship with God takes intentional time and effort. God has graciously given us His Word to know and love Him more – His character, His nature, His history, His promises, His plan, and His unsurpassed glory. Prayer allows us to communicate and connect with God, while aligning our hearts and minds with His holy purposes.

How could greater consistency and sincerity with Bible study and prayer impact your current circumstances?

In 1 Timothy 6:11-12, Paul advises,

> "But you, man of God, flee from all this, and pursue righteousness, godliness, faith, love, endurance and gentleness. Fight the good fight of the faith. Take hold of the eternal life to which you were called when you made your good confession in the presence of many witnesses."

To summarize, Paul calls his disciple Timothy to assess his habits against the truth of God's Word. His first command is to flee from whatever keeps him from living a godly life. He recommends Timothy adopt a war-time mentality and view surrender to God as the only way to achieve true victory. Paul calls his brother in Christ to not only stop doing the wrong things, but to pursue the right things through Christ-- godly faith, character, and practice.

To pursue "righteousness, godliness, faith, love, endurance and gentleness" is to follow Christ and to live out the will of God. However, the path of faithfulness is never an easy one. Humility, grace, and courage prove essential to "fight the good fight of the faith." You must see every day as a war for your soul, with the enemy fighting for your life, peace, perspective, and purpose. You must follow Christ, no matter the cost. As the late missionary Jim Elliot reminds us, "He is no fool who gives what he cannot keep to gain that which he cannot lose."

What habits do you need to flee? What keeps you from a deeper relationship with Jesus Christ?

What new habit do you want to implement in your life?

How has "training yourself to be godly" (1 Tim. 4:7) throughout the *Blueprint* **handbook impacted your life, purpose, and perspective?**

Congratulations on Completing *Blueprint*!

We pray you will continue to grow in your knowledge, understanding, and worship of God—our Creator, Sustainer, Savior, and Lord!

We would love to hear your story and celebrate your commitment to growing as a disciple of Christ! Please email welcomehomemission@gmail.com and share how *Blueprint* has helped you!

Thanks for choosing *Blueprint*!

Creeds

THE APOSTLES' CREED

I believe in God, the Father almighty,
    creator of heaven and earth.

I believe in Jesus Christ, his only Son, our Lord,
    who was conceived by the Holy Spirit
    and born of the virgin Mary.
    He suffered under Pontius Pilate,
    was crucified, died, and was buried;
    he descended to hell.
    The third day he rose again from the dead.
    He ascended to heaven
    and is seated at the right hand of God the Father almighty.
    From there he will come to judge the living and the dead.

I believe in the Holy Spirit,
    the holy catholic* church,
    the communion of saints,
    the forgiveness of sins,
    the resurrection of the body,
    and the life everlasting. Amen.

THE NICENE CREED

We believe in one God,
    the Father almighty,
    maker of heaven and earth,
    of all things visible and invisible.

And in one Lord Jesus Christ,
    the only Son of God,
    begotten from the Father before all ages,
        God from God,
        Light from Light,
        true God from true God,
    begotten, not made;
    of the same essence as the Father.
    Through him all things were made.
    For us and for our salvation
        he came down from heaven;
        he became incarnate by the Holy Spirit and the virgin Mary,
        and was made human.
        He was crucified for us under Pontius Pilate;
        he suffered and was buried.
        The third day he rose again, according to the Scriptures.
        He ascended to heaven
        and is seated at the right hand of the Father.
        He will come again with glory
        to judge the living and the dead.
        His kingdom will never end.

And we believe in the Holy Spirit,
    the Lord, the giver of life.
    He proceeds from the Father and the Son,
    and with the Father and the Son is worshiped and glorified.
    He spoke through the prophets.
    We believe in one holy catholic and apostolic church.
    We affirm one baptism for the forgiveness of sins.
    We look forward to the resurrection of the dead,
    and to life in the world to come. Amen.

Hymns

AMAZING GRACE (John Newton)

Amazing grace! How sweet the sound
That saved a wretch like me!
I once was lost, but now am found;
Was blind, but now I see.

'Twas grace that taught my heart to fear,
And grace my fears relieved;
How precious did that grace appear
The hour I first believed.

Through many dangers, toils and snares,
I have already come;
'Tis grace hath brought me safe thus far,
And grace will lead me home.

The Lord has promised good to me,
His Word my hope secures;
He will my Shield and Portion be,
As long as life endures.

Yea, when this flesh and heart shall fail,
And mortal life shall cease,
I shall possess, within the veil,
A life of joy and peace.

The earth shall soon dissolve like snow,
The sun forbear to shine;
But God, who called me here below,
Will be forever mine.

When we've been there ten thousand years,
Bright shining as the sun,
We've no less days to sing God's praise
Than when we'd first begun.

HOLY, HOLY, HOLY (Reginald Heber)

Holy, holy, holy! Lord God Almighty!
Early in the morning our song shall rise to Thee;
Holy, holy, holy, merciful and mighty!
God in three Persons, blessed Trinity!

Holy, holy, holy! All the saints adore Thee,
Casting down their golden crowns around the glassy sea;
Cherubim and seraphim falling down before Thee,
Who was, and is, and evermore shall be.

Holy, holy, holy! Though the darkness hide Thee,
Though the eye of sinful man Thy glory may not see;
Only Thou art holy; there is none beside Thee,
Perfect in pow'r, in love, and purity.

Holy, holy, holy! Lord God Almighty!
All Thy works shall praise Thy Name, in earth, and sky, and sea;
Holy, holy, holy; merciful and mighty!
God in three Persons, blessed Trinity!

HOW GREAT THOU ART (Carl Boberg)

O Lord, my God, when I in awesome wonder
Consider all the worlds Thy Hands have made
I see the stars, I hear the rolling thunder
Thy power throughout the universe displayed

Then sings my soul, my Saviour God, to Thee
How great Thou art, how great Thou art
Then sings my soul, my Saviour God, to Thee
How great Thou art, how great Thou art

And when I think of God, His Son not sparing
Sent Him to die, I scarce can take it in
That on the Cross, my burden gladly bearing
He bled and died to take away my sin

Then sings my soul, my Saviour God, to Thee
How great Thou art, how great Thou art
Then sings my soul, my Saviour God, to Thee
How great Thou art, how great Thou art

When Christ shall come with shout of acclamation
And lead me home, what joy shall fill my heart
Then I shall bow with humble adoration
And then proclaim, my God, how great Thou art

Then sings my soul, my Saviour God, to Thee
How great Thou art, how great Thou art
Then sings my soul, my Saviour God, to Thee
How great Thou art, how great Thou art

IT IS WELL WITH MY SOUL *(Horatio Spafford)*

When peace, like a river, attendeth my way,
When sorrows like sea billows roll;
Whatever my lot, Thou hast taught me to say,
It is well, it is well with my soul.

Refrain: It is well with my soul,
It is well, it is well with my soul.

Though Satan should buffet, though trials should come,
Let this blest assurance control,
That Christ hath regarded my helpless estate,
And hath shed His own blood for my soul.

My sin—oh, the bliss of this glorious thought!—
My sin, not in part but the whole,
Is nailed to the cross, and I bear it no more,
Praise the Lord, praise the Lord, O my soul!

For me, be it Christ, be it Christ hence to live:
If Jordan above me shall roll,
No pang shall be mine, for in death as in life
Thou wilt whisper Thy peace to my soul.

But, Lord, 'tis for Thee, for Thy coming we wait,
The sky, not the grave, is our goal;
Oh, trump of the angel! Oh, voice of the Lord!
Blessed hope, blessed rest of my soul!

And Lord, haste the day when the faith shall be sight,
The clouds be rolled back as a scroll;
The trump shall resound, and the Lord shall descend,
Even so, it is well with my soul.

THE SOLID ROCK (Edward Mote)

My hope is built on nothing less
Than Jesus' blood and righteousness;
I dare not trust the sweetest frame,
But wholly lean on Jesus' name.

Refrain: On Christ, the solid Rock, I stand;
All other ground is sinking sand,
All other ground is sinking sand.

When darkness veils His lovely face,
I rest on His unchanging grace;
In every high and stormy gale,
My anchor holds within the veil.

His oath, His covenant, His blood
Support me in the whelming flood;
When all around my soul gives way,
He then is all my hope and stay.

When He shall come with trumpet sound,
Oh, may I then in Him be found;
Dressed in His righteousness alone,
Faultless to stand before the throne.

12 Promises for "PEAK PERSEVERANCE"

"...In this world you will have trouble. But take heart! I have overcome the world."
John 16:33

Promise #1: God's Path
John 8:12

Promise #2: God's Presence
Hebrews 13:5(b)-6

Promise #3: God's Perseverance
Philippians 1:6

Promise #4: God's Purpose
Romans 8:28

Promise #5: God's Power
2 Corinthians 12:9

Promise #6: God's Provision
Matthew 6:32-33

Promise #7: God's People
Hebrews 3:13-14

Promise #8: God's Perspective
James 1:4-5

Promise #9: God's Peace
Philippians 4:6-7

Promise #10: God's Protection
2 Thessalonians 3:3

Promise #11: God's Perfection
Colossians 3:4

Promise #12: God's Prize
James 1:12

"7 TRUTHS TO TREASURE"

1. OWNERSHIP

Everything is God's, even our money.

"The earth is the Lord's, and everything in it, the world, and all who live in it; for he founded it on the seas and established it on the waters." Psalm 24:1-2

"The heavens are yours, and yours also the earth; you founded the world and all that is in it." Psalm 89:11

2. STEWARDSHIP

Everything we have is God's gift to us, to be used according to His will - for His glory, our own need, and the good of others.

"Do you not know that your bodies are temples of the Holy Spirit, who is in you, whom you have received from God? You are not your own; you were bought at a price. Therefore honor God with your bodies." 1 Corinthians 6:19-20

"And do not set your heart on what you will eat or drink; do not worry about it. For the pagan world runs after all such things, and your Father knows that you need them. But seek his kingdom, and these things will be given to you as well. Do not be afraid, little flock, for your Father has been pleased to give you the kingdom. Sell your possessions and give to the poor. Provide purses for yourselves that will not wear out, a treasure in heaven that will never fail, where no thief comes near and no moth destroys. For where your treasure is, there your heart will be also." Luke 11:29-34

3. RELATIONSHIP

A relationship with God through faith in Jesus Christ is the greatest gift, the most valuable treasure.

"The kingdom of heaven is like treasure hidden in a field. When a man found it, he hid it again, and then in his joy went and sold all he had and bought that field." Matthew 13:44

"Praise be to the God and Father of our Lord Jesus Christ, who has blessed us in the heavenly realms with every spiritual blessing in Christ." Ephesians 1:3

"In him we have redemption through his blood, the forgiveness of sins, in accordance with the riches of God's grace that he lavished on us." Ephesians 1:7-8[a]

"My goal is that they may be encouraged in heart and united in love, so that they may have the full riches of complete understanding, in order that they may know the mystery of God, namely, Christ, in whom are hidden all the treasures of wisdom and knowledge." Colossians 2:2-3

4. LORDSHIP

How we steward our money reflects who is the Lord of our life.

"For where your treasure is, there your heart will be also." Matthew 6:21

"No one can serve two masters. Either you will hate the one and love the other, or you will be devoted to the one and despise the other. You cannot serve both God and money." Matthew 6:24

" You have lived on earth in luxury and self-indulgence. You have fattened yourselves in the day of slaughter." James 5:5

5. HARDSHIP

The love of money leads to delusion, distraction, desperation, and destruction.

"Those who want to get rich fall into temptation and a trap and into many foolish and harmful desires that plunge people into ruin and destruction. For the love of money is a root of all kinds of evil. Some people, eager for money, have wandered from the faith and pierced themselves with many griefs." 1 Timothy 6:9-10

"Such are the paths of all who go after ill-gotten gain; it takes away the life of those who get it." Proverbs 1:19

" Whoever loves money never has enough; whoever loves wealth is never satisfied with their income. This too is meaningless." Ecclesiastes 5:10

6. WORSHIP

Christ-centered gratitude compels us to be content, regardless of circumstances, and generous, regardless of income.

"I know what it is to be in need, and I know what it is to have plenty. I have learned the secret of being content in any and every situation, whether well fed or hungry, whether living in plenty or in want. I can do all this through him who gives me strength." Philippians 4:12-13

"This is how we know what love is: Jesus Christ laid down his life for us. And we ought to lay down our lives for our brothers and sisters. If anyone has material possessions and sees a brother or sister in need but has no pity on them, how can the love of God be in that person? Dear children, let us not love with words or speech but with actions and in truth." 1 John 3:16-18

Luke 21:1-4 - And He looked up and saw the rich putting their gifts into the treasury, and He saw also a certain poor widow putting in two mites. So He said, "Truly I say to you that this poor widow has put in more than all; for all these out of their abundance have put in offerings for God, but she out of her poverty put in all the livelihood that she had."

7. CITIZENSHIP

This fallen world is not our forever home; therefore, God calls us to spend and invest our resources with an eternal perspective.

"For, as I have often told you before and now tell you again even with tears, many live as enemies of the cross of Christ. Their destiny is destruction, their god is their stomach, and their glory is in their shame. Their mind is set on earthly things. But our citizenship is in heaven. And we eagerly await a Savior from there, the Lord Jesus Christ," Philippians 3:18-20

"Do not store up for yourselves treasures on earth, where moths and vermin destroy, and where thieves break in and steal. But store up for yourselves treasures in heaven, where moths and vermin do not destroy, and where thieves do not break in and steal. For where your treasure is, there your heart will be also." Matthew 6:19-21

Made in the USA
Columbia, SC
25 June 2019